T0345681

1 **What makes a good friend? Write adjectives.**

I think a good friend is _____ .

2 **Look at the graph. Then read. What is a good friend like?**

Describing a good friend   by Emily Bower

This graph shows what the children in my class think a good friend is like.

The answers are from ten children: six boys and four girls. Here's what they think:

'Kind' has got the highest number, most of them prefer a friend who tries to help people and make them happy.

And 'bossy' has got the lowest number; they don't like someone telling them what to do all the time.

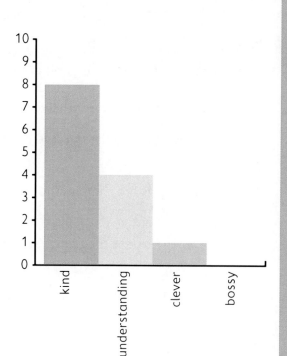

Eight children think a good friend is kind. Four think a good friend tries to 'understand' you with no questions about why you do or say something. Only one person thinks that a good friend is clever with good marks in exams.

And no one thinks that a 'bossy' person makes a good friend.

I agree with that! I think bossy people are very bad friends!

1 Describing a graph

3 **Read the text again. Then circle _True_ (T) or _False_ (F).**

1 Seven children think a good friend is kind.   T / F
2 Most children think a good friend is bossy.   T / F
3 One child thinks a good friend is clever.   T / F
4 Four children think a good friend is understanding.   T / F
5 More children think a good friend is clever than bossy.   T / F
6 Emily thinks bossy people make good friends.   T / F

4 **Read the text again. Then complete.**

1 The graph _____ what the children in Emily's class think about

   how a _____ friend is.

2 Four children think a good friend is _____ .

3 Eight children think a good friend is _____ .

4 No one thinks a _____ person makes a good friend.

5 Only one person thinks a good friend must be _____ .

5 **Read the text again. Then answer.**

1 How many boys are there in the class?

   _____ .

2 How many girls are there in the class?

   _____ .

3 Which word has got the highest number?

   _____ .

4 Which word has got the lowest number?

   _____ .

5 Which word has only got one vote?

   _____ .

6 **Unscramble. Then match with their opposites.**

1 sybso   **a** zaly

   _ _ _ _ _   _ _ _ _

2 typsro   **b** ktevaliat

   _ _ _ _ _ _   _ _ _ _ _ _ _ _ _

3 hsy   **c** dikn

   _ _ _   _ _ _ _

Remember!

An adjective comes before a noun.
a lovely girl
an intelligent doctor
a hard-working student

7 **Read. Then underline the adjectives.**

Alice is my best friend and she's an excellent tennis player. She's so sporty! I'm the opposite; I'm lazy! I never do any sport. But I like watching sport on TV!

Alice is also very clever and kind. If I can't do my homework, she always helps me. Well, she doesn't do my homework for me but she explains what I have to do. Her mum is also very friendly. And she's so talkative! Every time I go to their house, she talks and talks and talks. She's always excited about everything I do and wants to hear all my news! I'm never bored in Alice's house!

8 **Write (✔) or (✗). Then write correctly.**

1 inteligent ✗ _____
2 young ☐ _____
3 exited ☐ _____
4 lovley ☐ _____
5 helpful ☐ _____

9 **Write the adjectives. Then find and circle.**

1 Look at that baby! She's very c u t e .
2 He plays football every day. He's very s _ _ _ _ _ .
3 She's a very warm and f _ _ _ _ _ _ _ person.
4 He isn't old; he's y _ _ _ _ _ .
5 She always thinks about other people. She's very k _ _ _ _ .
6 When there is a problem, a friend is h _ _ _ _ _ _ .
7 It's my birthday! I'm so e _ _ _ _ _ _ _ !
8 This game isn't interesting. I'm b _ _ _ _ _ .

P	A	T	V	U	N	F	M	A	V	D	C
D	W	F	A	O	T	R	S	P	H	B	F
E	Z	R	Y	D	L	I	G	B	D	O	H
X	U	U	C	U	T	E	E	A	W	R	E
C	S	N	P	B	J	N	H	B	A	E	R
I	H	P	F	C	E	D	I	V	Q	D	S
T	K	G	O	S	Z	L	A	U	T	N	J
E	Q	I	R	R	D	Y	O	U	N	G	X
D	G	B	N	K	T	O	C	I	F	R	M
C	E	B	W	D	T	Y	Y	Y	B	A	Y
C	H	D	H	E	L	P	F	U	L	J	K
I	O	A	X	M	K	T	D	L	S	A	L

Describing a graph

10 **Describe the graph.**

- What does the graph show?
- Who are the answers from?
- What are the answers?
- Which word has got the highest/lowest number?
- Do you agree?

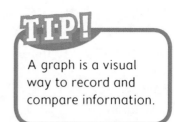

A graph is a visual way to record and compare information.

Describing a good friend by _____

_____

_____

_____

_____

_____

_____

_____

10
9
8
7
6
5
4
3
2
1
0

hard-working   lazy   talkative   helpful

My life

A blog entry

1 **Do you get pocket money? How much? How often? Write.**

_____ .

2 **Read. Would you do the washing up for extra money?**

_____ .

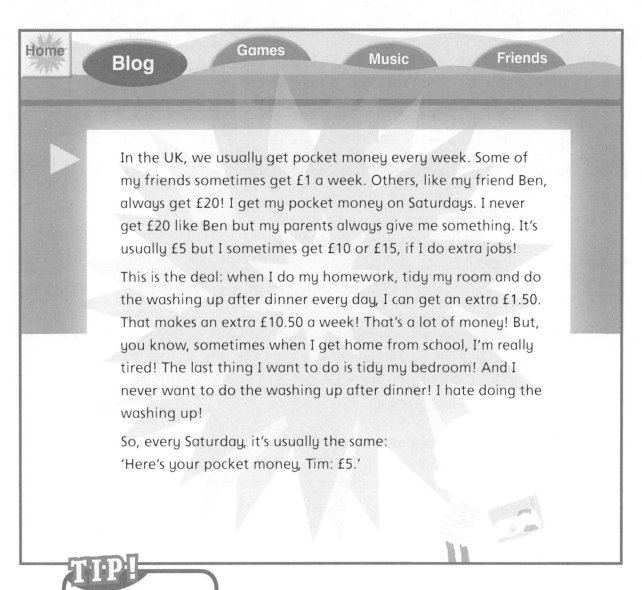

Home Blog Games Music Friends

In the UK, we usually get pocket money every week. Some of my friends sometimes get £1 a week. Others, like my friend Ben, always get £20! I get my pocket money on Saturdays. I never get £20 like Ben but my parents always give me something. It's usually £5 but I sometimes get £10 or £15, if I do extra jobs!

This is the deal: when I do my homework, tidy my room and do the washing up after dinner every day, I can get an extra £1.50. That makes an extra £10.50 a week! That's a lot of money! But, you know, sometimes when I get home from school, I'm really tired! The last thing I want to do is tidy my bedroom! And I never want to do the washing up after dinner! I hate doing the washing up!

So, every Saturday, it's usually the same:
'Here's your pocket money, Tim: £5.'

TIP!

Pocket money is what parents give their children for personal expenses.

3 **Read the text again. Then circle.**

1 Tim gets his pocket money on …

  a Fridays.

  b Saturdays.

  c Sundys.

2 Sometimes Tim doesn't tidy his room because he's …

  a lazy.

  b tired.

  c late for school.

3 Tim hates …

  a doing his homework.

  b making his bed.

  c doing the washing up.

4 **Read the text again. Then circle** *True* **(T) or** *False* **(F).**

1 Tim gets pocket money every week.   T / F

2 Ben's parents always give him £5 a week.   T / F

3 Tim is always tired when he gets home from school.   T / F

4 If Tim does all the jobs, he can get an extra £10.50. T / F

5 Tim usually gets £15.50 on Saturdays.   T / F

5 **Match. Then find the words in Tim's blog and underline them.**

1 get   **a** my homework

2 do   **b** pocket money

3 tidy   **c** extra jobs

4 do   **d** my room

6 **Read the answers. Then write questions about Tim.**

1 _____ ?

  Every week.

2 _____ ?

  On Saturday.

3 _____ ?

  Usually £5.

4 _____ ?

  He tidies his room, does the washing up …

5 _____ ?

  When he gets home from school.

7 **Write a, e, i, o or u. Then match.**

1 sn _a_ ck

2 ch _ c _ l _ t _

3 s _ g _ r

4 fl _ _ r

5 b _ tt _ r

6 s _ lt

a We use this to make bread.

b We put this in coffee to make it sweet.

c We often put this in food to make it taste better.

d This is brown and sweet.

e We often put this on bread.

f We often eat this after breakfast and before lunch.

8 **Read. Then complete.**

a test   ~~my bed~~   my homework   out the rubbish   washing up

18ᵗʰ • March

I always make ¹ _my bed_ before I go to school. Sometimes I do the ² _____ after dinner and I always help my parents to take ³ _____. I never do ⁴ _____ when I get home from school but today I must revise for ⁵ _____. But I'm too tired!

9 **Write about Fiona. Use always, usually, sometimes and never.**

	Monday	Tuesday	Wednesday	Thursday	Friday
tidy her bedroom	✔	✔	✔	✔	
do the washing up					
make her bed	✔	✔	✔	✔	✔
meet her friends				✔	✔

1 Fiona usually _____.

2 _____.

3 _____.

4 _____.

2 A blog entry

 Underline seven more mistakes. Then correct.

During the week, I <u>gett</u> up at 7.30 a.m. to go to school. At the weekend I usualy get up at 9.00. I somtimes read for an hour and then I lissen to music. After breckfast, we go to the supermarket to get the shoping for the week. I alweys look at the magazines and meet my parents on the way out. In the afternoon, I meet my frends and we play football. I love the weekend!

1   get _____   5   _____

2   _____   6   _____

3   _____   7   _____

4   _____   8   _____

 Write a blog entry about pocket money.

- Do you get pocket money?
- How much do you usually get?
- When do you usually get it?
- Do you have to do any jobs to get it? If yes, what jobs do you have to do?
- What do you usually do with your pocket money?

TIP!

A blog (short for Web Log) is a website where you can write information ordered by date.

Home   Blog   Games   Music   Friends

1 **What do you like doing in your free time? Write.**

_____.

2 **Read. What are the children writing about?**

_____.

1

I'm Rob. In my free time I like playing football and volleyball. I often meet my friends after school and we play football in the park. My friends say I'm the best player in the school. I'm also captain of the school football team! I'm very good at playing sports but I also love watching them on TV – I always follow the football scores of my favourite team on TV!

2

My name's Marcela and I love reading, so in my free time, I usually... read! I don't like watching TV or playing video games. I also like going to the reading club at weekends - it's great fun! I'm also very good at writing - I want to write a book one day. Last month I wrote a short story for the school writing contest and guess what? I won!

3

My name's Harry and I love music. I love listening to music, playing music and singing, of course! But I don't like dancing because I'm not very good at it. I play the drums and the piano. Next year I want to learn to play the guitar. At the weekend, my friends and I often sing karaoke. Music's great!

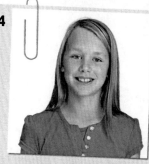

4

I'm Gwyneth and I do lots of things in my free time. I like drawing, watching TV, playing video games and going shopping.

I often play video games with my brother - he likes them, too. He also likes chess, but I don't because I'm not good at it. I never win! At the weekend I usually go shopping with my friend, Ann. Then, we usually have lunch together and in the afternoon we play video games with my brother.

3 Describing interests and hobbies

3 **Read the texts again. Then match.**

1 Rob likes   a music.
2 Marcela likes   b video games.
3 Harry likes   c football.
4 Gwyneth likes   d reading.

4 **Read the texts again. Then circle.**

1 Rob likes ...   2 Rob is captain of the school ...
   a football and tennis.   a football team.
   b tennis and volleyball.   b volleyball team.
   c football and volleyball.   c basketball team.

3 Last month Marcela wrote a ...   4 At the weekend, Gwyneth goes ...
   a song.   a shopping.
   b story.   b singing.
   c poem.   c playing the drums.

5 Gwyneth doesn't like ...   6 Harry plays ...
   a drawing.   a the drums.
   b chess.   b the guitar.
   c watching TV.   c the piano.

5 **Read the texts again. Then answer.**

1 Where do Rob and his friends often play football?

   _____.

2 What does Marcela want to do?

   _____.

3 What instruments can Harry play?

   _____.

4 When does Gwyneth usually go shopping?

   _____.

6 **Look. Then match.**

1 sing   a music
2 play   b the drums
3 have   c lunch
4 listen to   d karaoke
5 go   e books
6 read   f shopping

7 **Write *a*, *e*, *i*, *o* or *u*. Then match.**

1 s _ ng _ ng k _ r _ _ k _

2 r _ ll _ rbl _ d _ ng

3 _ ct _ ng

4 d _ v _ ng

5 r _ nn _ ng r _ c _ s

6 pl _ y _ ng v _ d _ _ g _ m _ s

a  b   c   d  e   f

8 **Unscramble. Then match.**

1 resco

_ _ _ _ _ _

2 hgapr

_ _ _ _ _ _

3 etam

_ _ _ _

4 ealctucla

_ _ _ _ _ _ _ _ _

a  b  c  d

A a visual way to record and compare information

B the number of points a team has got

C use of numbers to find the correct answer to something

D a group of people that play together in a sport

3 Describing interests and hobbies

Remember!

I like / love / enjoy / don't like playing video games.
I prefer playing video games to watching TV.
I would rather play video games than watch TV.

9 **Write four things you like doing in your free time.**

_____

_____

_____

_____

10 **Write about your hobbies and interests.**

- What do you like doing in your free time?
- When / How often do you do these things?
- Who do you do them with?
- What are you good at?

_____

_____

_____

_____

_____

_____

_____

_____

_____

_____

_____

Around the world

A travel diary entry

1 Do you write a diary about your trips?

_____ .

2 Read. Then write. Where are the children?

1 Mira _____ .

2 Johnny _____ .

3 Lucy _____ .

Mira

My travel diary:
Colombia, South
America
Friday, 14th June, Bogota

We are staying in a small hotel in Bogota.
It's very warm. The people are very friendly
and our rooms are very comfortable.
Bogota is the capital of Colombia. It is
in the Andes mountains. We can do lots of
things here: we can go climbing, trekking and,
of course, diving in the Caribbean. I can't
wait! And the food is delicious - lots of
seafood with hot spices. My favourite!

Sunday 6th May Cairo
My travel diary:
Egypt, Africa
I can't believe it!
I'm in, Egypt! I'm in
Africa! And I can see
the River Nile from my
window! But I can't
see any crocodiles.
There are lots of
crocodiles in the Nile,
so I can't go swimming.
Next week we're going
to Alexandria. I'm so
excited!

Johnny

My travel diary –
Greece, Europe
Tuesday, 14th August,
Athens

Here I am in Greece!
Wow! It's beautiful!
The sea is so blue! I'm
in a hotel in Athens,
the capital of Greece.
It's big and noisy!

Tomorrow we're going
to Samos, one of the
Greek islands. I can't
wait! There are lots
of beaches and small
villages on the island.
Our hotel is next
to the beach. Three
weeks of swimming!
Fantastic!

Lucy

4 A travel diary entry

3 **Read the texts again. Then answer.**

1 Who is going to Samos?

_____ .

2 Who can go diving in the Caribbean?

_____ .

3 Who is going to Alexandria?

_____ .

4 Who likes seafood?

_____ .

4 **Read the texts again. Then match.**

1	friendly people	**a**	the River Nile
2	crocodiles	**b**	Greece
3	islands	**c**	Samos
4	small villages	**d**	Bogota

5 **Read the texts again. Then circle.**

1 Mira thinks …
  a the food isn't very good.
  b the people are friendly.
  c Bogota is noisy.

2 Johnny is …
  a worried.
  b bored.
  c excited.

3 Tomorrow Lucy is going …
  a to a Greek island.
  b to Athens.
  c home.

4 Athens is …
  a big and noisy.
  b small and noisy.
  c small and quiet.

6 **Read the texts again. Then write in the grid.**

Colombia   crocodiles   Cairo   the Andes   spicy food   Samos   Egypt   swimming
Caribbean   Alexandria   Greece   River Nile   Bogota   Athens   noisy

South America	Africa	Europe
_____	_____	_____
_____	_____	_____
_____	_____	_____
_____	_____	_____

7 **Unscramble. Then match.**

1 ytrcfao	**2** dyiprma	**3** olovnca	**4** ecav	**5** ytci	**6** etauts
_ _ _ _ _ _	_ _ _ _ _ _	_ _ _ _ _ _	_ _ _ _	_ _ _ _	_ _ _ _ _

a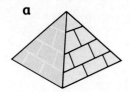

b

c

d

e

f

8 **Read. Then complete.**

hills   air   lakes   planet   sky

19th August

I am in Argentina. I am in the Andes. The ¹_____
is very clean. There are lots of high mountains and smaller
²_____ . There are lots of ³_____ where we
can go fishing. The ⁴_____ above is blue, blue, blue!
There are lots of trees and plants and animals here, too. What
an amazing place our ⁵_____ is!

9 **Unscramble. Find eight countries.**

1 eakro _ _ _ _ _

2 tepyg _ _ _ _ _

3 aatulrsia _ _ _ _ _ _ _ _ _

4 anringtea _ _ _ _ _ _ _ _ _

5 cmieox _ _ _ _ _ _

6 cihan _ _ _ _ _

7 padoln _ _ _ _ _ _

8 atiyl _ _ _ _ _

4 A travel diary entry

Remember!

We use capital letters for countries and names of places.

France   Spain   the Amazon Rainforest   the Andes

10 **Read and write ✔ or ✗. Then correct.**

1 the river nile ☐ _____

2 the andes in colombia ☐ _____

3 the Pyramids of egypt ☐ _____

4 Spain ☐ _____

11 **Write your own travel diary.**

• Where are you?

• What is the country / city / town / island like?

• Where are you staying?

• What can you do / see there?

T·I·P!
You can use a diary to write about personal activities, ideas or feelings during a trip or holiday.

Shopping

Adverts

1 **Where can you find adverts for clothes and accessories? Write.**

_____.

2 **Read. What do you think they should buy?**

_____.

Molly and John are twins. It's their birthday soon. They want to buy their birthday presents. Their mum and dad said they can spend up to £50 each.

They looked in some magazines and saw the following adverts. They are very excited. Some of the prices are too expensive but there are some good prices too that are much cheaper.

Molly wants some new clothes. She likes the pink tracksuit but she also wants some jeans and a new shirt. John would rather have accessories. He likes the watch but it's too expensive. The wallet is cheaper.

They work out how many things they can buy with their birthday money.

TRACKSUIT, pink, £40
For a girl 1.60 m tall
Photo on page 63
Tel: 775-846-5160, Amy

WALLET, new
Brown leather, only £20!
Tel: 563-558-9672
stephen-b@fdinternet.com

SHIRT, used, £5
White, baggy,
two pockets
For boys Size: small
Tel: 775-877-8800
Keith

GLOVES
3 pairs for £15
Red, green and black
Call Emma at 458-967-5894

JEANS, used, £10
Blue, tight
For girls; Size: medium
Photo on page 67
Tel: 699-856-4030, Rebecca
becky_smith@fdinternet.com

WATCH, new
Modern, black, for boys
Down from £150 to £65.50!
Call or email Fred   743-001-6644
fred_3451@ntdconline.com

UMBRELLA, new
Yellow, **£14**   Call Heather at 775-895-5550

3   **Read the texts again. Then match.**

1	pink	**a**	umbrella
2	brown	**b**	tracksuit
3	green	**c**	jeans
4	baggy	**d**	watch
5	modern	**e**	wallet
6	tight	**f**	gloves
7	yellow	**g**	shirt

4   **Read the texts again. Then match.**

1	watch	**a**	£5
2	wallet	**b**	£10
3	jeans	**c**	£14
4	gloves	**d**	£15
5	umbrella	**e**	£20
6	tracksuit	**f**	£40
7	shirt	**g**	£65.50

5   **Read the texts again. Then circle.**

1   The brown leather wallet is from …
   a   Rebecca.
   b   Stephen.
   c   Fred.

2   Emma's gloves are …
   a   very colourful.
   b   in a different colour each pair.
   c   made from leather.

3   Rebecca's used jeans …
   a   are blue and tight.
   b   are red, green and black.
   c   are baggy.

4   Keith is selling …
   a   an umbrella.
   b   a pair of gloves.
   c   a used shirt.

5   Fred's watch is …
   a   used.
   b   new.
   c   a present for his mum.

6   Amy's tracksuit is …
   a   for a very tall girl.
   b   for a boy.
   c   for a girl 1.6 m tall.

6 **Look at the pictures. Then write.**

1

2

3

4

tracksuit _____   _____   _____   _____

5

6

7

8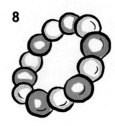

_____   _____   _____   _____

7 **Unscramble. Then match the opposites.**

1 vinexesep   _ _ _ _ _ _ _ _ _   **a** baggy

2 dol-hionfedsa   _ _ _ - _ _ _ _ _ _ _ _ _   **b** modern

3 higtt   _ _ _ _ _   **c** cheap

8 **Read. Then complete.**

assistant	change	department	label	much	shopping

1 **A:** Let's go _____ on Saturday.

     B: Yes! Let's go to that new _____ store!

2 **A:** The shop _____ was very friendly.

     B: Yes, but I gave her £5 and she didn't give me my _____!

3 **A:** How _____ is that jacket?

     B: Let's look at the _____. Oh! It's £124!

5 Adverts

An advert is clear and simple. It only gives important information.

9 Write eight things you have but don't need.

_____ _____

_____ _____

_____ _____

_____ _____

TIP!

An advert is a picture or words describing something that is for sale.

10 Choose four things from Activity 9 and write adverts for them. Draw a picture for each one.

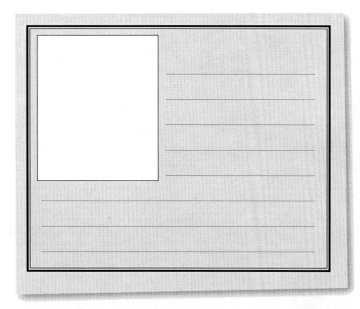

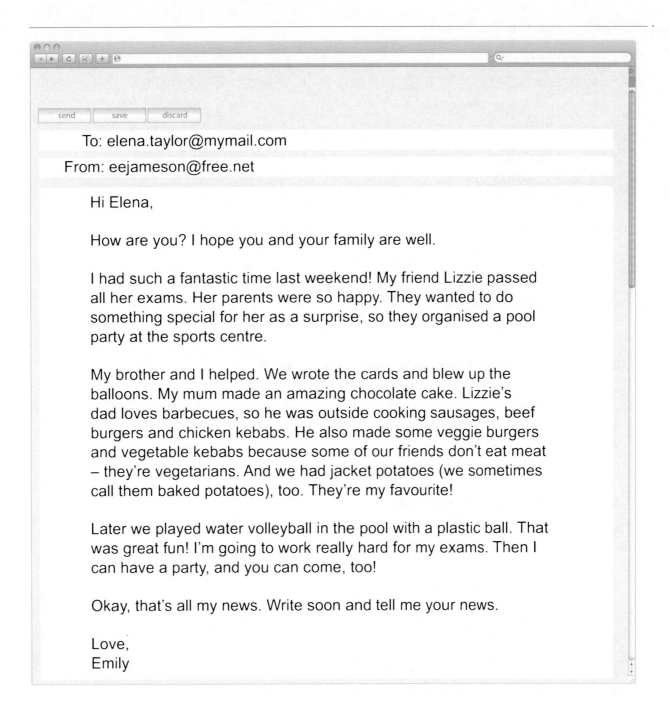

Party time
An email

 6

1 Do you like parties? Why? / Why not? Write.

_____.

2 Read. Then write. When was the party?

_____.

send   save   discard

To: elena.taylor@mymail.com

From: eejameson@free.net

Hi Elena,

How are you? I hope you and your family are well.

I had such a fantastic time last weekend! My friend Lizzie passed all her exams. Her parents were so happy. They wanted to do something special for her as a surprise, so they organised a pool party at the sports centre.

My brother and I helped. We wrote the cards and blew up the balloons. My mum made an amazing chocolate cake. Lizzie's dad loves barbecues, so he was outside cooking sausages, beef burgers and chicken kebabs. He also made some veggie burgers and vegetable kebabs because some of our friends don't eat meat – they're vegetarians. And we had jacket potatoes (we sometimes call them baked potatoes), too. They're my favourite!

Later we played water volleyball in the pool with a plastic ball. That was great fun! I'm going to work really hard for my exams. Then I can have a party, and you can come, too!

Okay, that's all my news. Write soon and tell me your news.

Love,
Emily

6 An email

3 **Read the text again. Then match.**

1	Emily	**a**	made a chocolate cake.
2	Emily's mum	**b**	passed her exams.
3	Emily's brother	**c**	loves jacket potatoes.
4	Lizzie's parents	**d**	blew up balloons.
5	Lizzie's dad	**e**	loves barbecues.
6	Lizzie	**f**	organised the surprise party.

4 **Read the text again. Then circle.**

1 Emily is writing to …

    a a friend.

    b someone she doesn't know.

    c her grandmother.

2 Lizzie's parents organised the party because …

    a it was Lizzie's birthday.

    b Lizzie loves parties.

    c Lizzie passed her exams.

3 The party was …

    a in the garden.

    b at the sports centre.

    c at Lizzie's house.

4 Emily's favourite food is …

    a sausages.

    b veggie burgers.

    c jacket potatoes.

5 Emily wants to work hard for her exams because …

    a she wants to see Elena.

    b she wants a party like Lizzie's.

    c she loves jacket potatoes.

5 **Read the text again. Then circle *True* (T) or *False* (F).**

1	Emily's brother helped, too.	T / F
2	Emily's mum made some ice cream.	T / F
3	All of Lizzie and Emily's friends eat meat.	T / F
4	Emily played volleyball at the party.	T / F

6 **Read the text again. Then answer.**

1 Who wrote the email?

_____ .

2 Where did they play volleyball?

_____ .

3 What did the vegetarians eat?

_____ .

4 How did Emily and her brother help with the party?

_____ .

7 **Read. Then complete.**

| ate | brought | came | gave (x2) | had (x3) | made | met | sang | went |

It was my friend Debbie's birthday yesterday. We ¹ _____ to a pizza restaurant near my house. We all ² _____ at the restaurant. Jake, Debbie's cousin, ³ _____ with us, too. I ⁴ _____ a present and a card for her. I ⁵ _____ her a beautiful pink and white necklace. I ⁶ _____ the necklace myself! And Jake ⁷ _____ her a book. We ⁸ _____ lots of food. I ⁹ _____ a four-cheese pizza. For dessert, we all ¹⁰ _____ ice-cream. Then we ¹¹ _____ Happy Birthday! We all ¹² _____ a really great time!

8 **Write the dates.**

1 21 / 6   twenty-first of June _____

2 30 / 9   _____

3 23 / 2   _____

4 25 / 8   _____

5 1 / 7   _____

9 **Sort.**

| April | January | February | March | May | November | October |

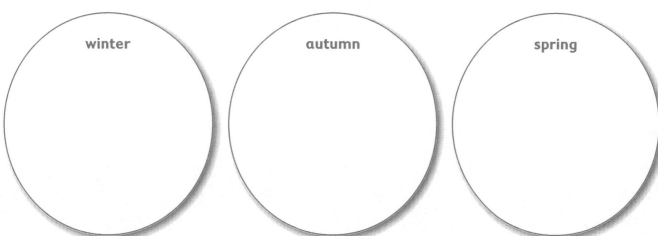

winter   autumn   spring

6 An email

10 **Write an email to a friend. Tell them about a party you had.**

- When / Where was the party?
- Why did you have the party?
- Who came?
- What did you do?
- How was the food / music?
- Did you have a good time?

1 **Have you got rules at your school? Which ones?**

_____

_____

2 **Read. Does Maria think school rules are a good thing? What do you think?**

_____

_____

Are school rules a good thing?

In my school we have lots of rules and I think this is right.

First, there are usually a lot of children in a school. In some countries, there are often over thirty children in a class. In other countries, there are over a hundred children in a class. It's important to have some rules so that everyone can work together safely. For example, going from one classroom to another or going up and down the stairs.

Second, rules help us to learn more about life outside school. We learn Maths, Music, Geography, Science, etc but we also learn what we can and can't do. This is interesting too! We learn how to talk to different people and to respect their ideas. We also learn what will happen if we do something we shouldn't do!

Third, rules help us to work and learn how to do things in a specific period of time. They help us to organise our lives so there is time to work and to relax. Sometimes the lesson takes longer because someone is talking or playing around. I don't think this is helpful for anyone!

In conclusion, I think rules are good. What do you think? What rules do you have in your school? Should there be more rules or less?

TIP!

- When you write an argument you present your ideas about something in a convincing way.
- A paragraph is a collection of lines about the same idea. We use them to present our ideas clearly.

3 **Read the text again. Then circle.**

1 Maria thinks rules are good for ...

   a helping people.

   b making classrooms quiet.

   c keeping the classroom and school safe.

2 In some countries, there are ...

   a more than a hundred children in a school.

   b fewer than thirty children in a class.

   c many children in one classroom.

3 Maria thinks lessons take longer when ...

   a there are no rules.

   b some children aren't working.

   c the class gets extra homework.

4 School rules help us ...

   a to respect other people's ideas.

   b to talk to other people.

   c to learn more about life outside school.

4 **Find the words or expressions in the text.**

1 These help you to organise your life.

_____.

2 Where you attend lessons in school.

_____.

3 The opposite of inside.

_____.

4 You need to use a calculator for this subject.

_____.

5 **Find the main ideas. Then match.**

1 First paragraph

2 Second paragraph

3 Third paragraph

a Learning to respect other ideas

b Helping to organize our lives

c Working together

6 **Read the text again. Then answer.**

1 How can people work together safely?

_____.

2 What does Maria think is interesting?

_____.

3 Do rules help us with our time?

_____.

4 What does Maria think is not helpful for anyone?

_____.

7 **Unscramble. Then match the opposites.**

1 igobrn _ _ _ _ _ _ _

2 liftifcdu _ _ _ _ _ _ _ _ _

3 ayrcs _ _ _ _ _

a funny

b interesting

c easy

8 **Write the school subjects.**

1

_____

2

_____

3

_____

4

_____

5

_____

6

_____

9 **Read. Then match.**

1 Glue is

2 Scissors are

3 A storyboard is

4 A character is

a a way to tell a story with pictures.

b a person in a story.

c something you need to stick things.

d something you use to cut things.

Remember!

Start a new paragraph for every new idea.

10 **Write about rules in your school / home.**

- What are the rules in your school / home?
- Why do you think they exist?
- Do you think they are good or bad?
- What other rules would you make?

1 In your country, do you have special days to celebrate different cultures? What do you do? Write.

_____

_____

2 Read. What is the text about?

_____

Egypt

Argentina

Brazil

Great Britain

China

International Day

One of the best days of the school year is International Day. It's a really special day because there are lots of exciting events for everyone in the school. A lot of nationalities from all over the world are present.

This year, International Day was on the 3rd of February. Each class had a country and all the children in that class – with their parents and teachers – worked together to decorate their classroom with pictures and maps from different countries (Brazil, Colombia, Egypt, Japan ...) and posters of important people from that country (astronaut, footballer, painter ...). Other rooms had displays of traditional costumes and showed DVDs of national dances. In the main hall, there were typical foods: Chinese, Spanish, Australian ...

The younger children had a special passport. They took this to each classroom and had to find out information about the country. Then they got a special stamp in the passport. There was a prize for the passport with the most stamps. There were also more prizes.
The first prize was a trip for two people to Canada!

The day ended with a concert with students, teachers and parents singing a song or playing musical instruments from 'their' country. It was amazing!

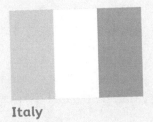

Italy

3 **Read the text again. Then circle.**

1 International Day is special because …
a there are different kinds of food.
b there are special events.
c it's in February.

2 The food was in the …
a classrooms.
b playground.
c hall.

3 The younger children's passport had …
a a special stamp in it.
b questions for the children to answer.
c lots of pictures.

4 At the end of the day, teachers and parents …
a sang or played musical instruments.
b played games.
c decorated the classrooms.

4 **Read the text again. Then circle *True* (T) or *False* (F).**

1 Younger students never take part in the events.   T / F
2 There were maps in the main hall.   T / F
3 There was food from many different countries.   T / F
4 All the children had a passport.   T / F
5 There were pictures in some classrooms.   T / F
6 The last activity was the concert.   T / F

5 **Match. Then find these words in the text and underline them.**

1 special   a costumes
2 traditional   b instruments
3 first   c passport
4 musical   d prize

6 **Read the answers. Then write questions.**

1 _____ ?

Because there are lots of exciting events.

2 _____ ?

All the children in the school, the teachers and the parents.

3 _____ ?

On the 3rd February.

4 _____ ?

In the main hall.

5 _____ ?

They had a special passport.

6 _____ ?

There were typical foods.

7 **Write (✔) or (✗). Then correct.**

1 Argeninian ☐ _____

2 Greek ☐ _____

3 Astralian ☐ _____

4 Corean ☐ _____

5 Pollish ☐ _____

6 Spanish ☐ _____

8 **Read. Then write.**

1 Someone who works with teeth.   _ e _ _ _ _ _ _

2 Someone who writes articles for newspapers   _ _ u _ _ _ _ _ _ _

3 Someone who works in a kitchen.   _ _ o _

4 Someone who works with cars.   _ _ _ h _ _ _ _

5 Someone who plays in films.   _ c _ _ _ _

6 Someone who travels into space.   _ s _ _ _ _ _ _ _

9 **Write the words in order. Start with the shortest period of time.**

| day | hour | minute | month | season | week | weekend | year |

1 _____   5 _____

2 _____   6 _____

3 _____   7 _____

4 _____   8 _____

10 **Look at the pictures. Then write the jobs.**

1 _____   2 _____   3 _____

4 _____   5 _____   6 _____

Remember!

A sentence starts with a capital letter. Names also start with a capital letter.
There are lots of rivers in England. The River Thames is the longest.

11 **Read. Then punctuate.**

last week we went on a school
trip to the tower of london we
left school at 9:15 and arrived at
tower bridge at 10:30 the coach
journey took a long time because
there was a lot of traffic on the
road we were really excited when
we arrived at the tower

Last week we

12 **Write an article about a special day at your school for the school magazine.**

- When is it?
- What happens every year?
- Who takes part in the event(s)?
- What happened last year?

An article is a piece of writing in a magazine on a particular subject, usually based on real events.